Black-Capped Chickadees

Messengers of Good News

Photos and Poems
by
Dwayne Cole

Soul of the Universe

As I contemplate in nature,
feeding black-capped chickadees,
I feel the Soul of the universe.
I celebrate beauty, wonder, goodness,
love, and kindness.

I especially feel these values
in alpenglow sunrises and sunsets,
as heart songs sing my soul awake.
As I contemplate my soul is one
with the world soul, the heart of everything.

Oh, joy of feeding
Black-capped chickadees heart seeds
Everything is music

Feeding chickadees
The universe is singing
Nature is alive

Poetic Importance of Feeling

In each visit of chickadees,
I feel the universe incarnating itself in beauty.
The eyes convey this spinning universe.

Becoming one with chickadees is an inter-connective activity that gives value to all of nature and inspires poetic ecology— tenderly preserving and saving the only world we have for our existence.

In the little chickadees we see a hunger for life, a hunger to propagate, to live. This is nature unfurling itself, revealing its wonder. In this mirror of nature I see my life unfolding in beauty and wonder. This oneness with nature is wrapped in my chickadee poems. The result is enlivenment and a deep sense of gratitude.

The dead of winter
Feeding little chickadees
World soul is alive

D. Cole

Black-capped chickadees are small birds that are 4 to 5 inches long with a wing span of 8 inches. They have small rounded bodies, and only weigh 10-12 grams. Some visit my deck and eat sunflower heart seeds from my hand all year round. They survive -40 degree temperatures in our Alaska winters by fluffing their feathers into a down sleeping bag and hanging out in a hollow tree or snow tunnel.

Whirligig Magic
Bringing joy to my day
Fluttering my heart

Good News

Chickadees are viewed positively
by many cultures. They are a symbol
of truth, good luck, and success.

Seeing their beauty and grace
one can believe this and more.
I am happy just sitting on my deck,
and watching them eat my sunflower seeds

Chickadees bring good luck.
Angel wings to inspire.

Moving the world closer
to beauty, goodness, and love.

Chickadee, come and light on me,
fill my life with bright wings.

Chickadees are poems
Messengers from unknown realms
Bring the gift of Peace

Wings catching sun fire
Chickadees light up my life
Good luck charm for sure

My wish for all lovers of nature—

Coming to say Hi
Bringing you Good News
With loving eyes

My philosophical bent led me for 50 years
as a minister in churches and as
an instructor in college and seminary classes,
to see the big picture—
World view and how we relate to the world.

Retired and living in Alaska
for the last twelve years,
I have gone into the beauty of the mountains
to be still and contemplate—

Paying attention to the small things:
the small black-capped chickadees,
nuthatches, and redpolls reveal the wonder of evolution.
I cup a single wildflower and see
the essence of the universe.

The gift of contemplation
is that in the small things
I see the large picture more clearly.
I see the God myth of Genesis as the world soul,
as Kindness, in all things and for all things,
in us and for us, luring us to become our best selves.
Meeting each entity with a tender care,
that nothing is lost. In the beauty of nature,
I see an enduring love for all things.

My world view grows to understand
all things connected and interrelated.
In these solitary moments I feel at home—
At home with beauty, goodness, and tenderness.
The Myth becomes reality.
My soul sings alleluia, alleluia!

Black capped chickadees
Love sunflower heart seeds
They bring me glee

I love summer time
Feeding chickadees heart seeds
The best time of all
Heaven's light glowing in wings
My heart joyfully sings

One will never forget
the first time a chickadee
lights in your hand

(Love is keeping dish clean,
Washing often with water and bleach.
Washing hands before and after they eat
from your hand to keep from spreading germs)

Bird/Human Behavior

After closely observing the birds
that visit the saucer of seeds
on my deck in Anchorage,
I have come to this conclusion—
If humans could grow feathers and wings
few would be as wise and resourceful
as the little chickadees.
If you put the human intellect
in birds they would all fly like bats—
Upside down and backwards.

One chickadee can store up to 1,000 seeds a day,
thousands in one season, to carry them through
the harsh Alaska temperatures that can reach
40 below zero. They sleep in tree cavities
and snow tunnels, fluff their feathers
into down sleeping bags and live for another day.
They survive by their own adaptability
and creativity, without any help from humans.
However, our destruction of the environment,
makes it harder for their survival.

We have the expression,
"Bird brain," meaning—
A person who lacks intelligence
or who makes bad decisions.

This expression is an insult to resourceful birds.
In fact, if you put the human brain
in birds they would all fly upside down
and backwards like bats!

Illumined by sunlight
Spreading wings in gratitude
Black cap pulled around ears
Black bib draped around neck
Heaven opens with angels singing

Loving eyes looked at me intently,
while tweeting a secret about a secret.
Friends keep secrets.

When many birds migrate to warmer climes, I pull out my favorite pictures and share with my "Birds of Alaska" friends. The last three photos above are my favorite chickadee photos and why I love them so—

Chickadees bring luck
On wings of inspiration
Beauty is bonus

In social isolation, my company is the adventurous spinning universe—I see in the bright eyes of birds coming to Alaska from different parts of the world. **Those eyes take me all the way back to wonder.** Beauty fills each day with adventurous discovery, as I read about a new bird photo. Reading shapes my dreams. My days are filled with taking photos of beautiful Alaska, reading, and writing. (The phrase, "social isolation," has many meanings for me: COVID pandemic.)

A translucent jewel
Chickadee in flight
Bird lover's delight

On cold nights when temperatures dip as low as -20, the chickadees sleep in hollow trees or snow tunnels. They fluff their feathers into a down sleeping bag and quiver to keep warm. This burns a lot of energy. Upon waking they have to find food soon or suffer from starvation. They can remember numerous places where they stored food for these times.

Snow keeps piling up
Chickadees need food to survive
Seeds keep them alive

Snow is falling
Chickadees come calling
Kindness wins the day

Chickadee Sonnet

Black-capped chickadees are such fun
Intent on stashing winter seeds
Feathers of hope, illumined by the sun.
Snowfall has just begun indeed.

Gather as many as you wish.
Devour to meet your needs.
High on my list is filling your dish
with sunflower heart seeds.

I'll never forget the wondrous feeling
the first time you landed in my hand.
You sent my heart reeling.

As long as you keep lighting in my hand,
I will write poems of love and kindness.
Your love is as true as a wedding band.

Action Sermon

Chickadees
stay in Alaska all year long
Store seeds for winter song

One little chickadee
can store 1,000 seeds a day
This is nature's way

If I can keep them
from suffering hunger pain
I'll not live in vain.

In social isolation from COVID, my company is the adventurous spinning universe I see in the bright eyes of the many little birds coming to Alaska from different parts of the world. Each day is filled with adventurous discovery. As the great RBG once said, "Reading is the key that opens doors to many good things in life. Reading shaped my dreams, and more reading helped me make my dreams come true." My days are filled with taking photos of beautiful Alaska, reading, and writing poems inspired by those photos.

Temperature at 24 degrees
Overhead clear blue skies
Chickadees knocking at my door
With black cap down around eyes

With wings all aglow
Chickadees put on art show
Embrace the beauty

Little Chickadees
Like a child finding a toy
Leaping for joy!

Faith, hope, and love
a black-capped chickadee
Eating from your hand

Winter snow is piling deep
on mountain peak

Little chickadees are active these days
storing seeds for this is nature's ways

If I can save them from hunger pain
I shall not live my life in vain

Oh let me songs raise
on wings of praise

Like a child with toy
Leaping for joy!

Times of pandemic
Require furious dancing
Alleluia!

Saint Francis preached to the birds.
I feed the birds and preach to the cats—
Thou shalt not eat my little song birds!

Be Kind

As most of my friends know
I try to live and write
from a spirit of kindness

This spirit is fueled by
my contemplative lifestyle
Walking in the beauty of Alaska

Observing a mother moose
Nuzzling her new born twins

Nuthatches and chickadees
eating sunflower heart seeds
from my hand

This meditative spirit
has led me to largely stay out of
heated political discussions

Tomorrow when the sun rises
on a new day
I will try to be kind

Chickadee Tanka

In golden sunrise
Little chickadee's eyes zing
My heart softly sings—
Mother Nature cares for birds
And she cares for you and me

Chickadee Glee

In times of social isolation
Chickadees bring jubilation
Thank you my little friends

Little chickadees
have come through molting, shining.
Ready for snow days.

Chickadees of hope
Messengers of love

Chimes of heaven ring
Angelic choirs sing

Hearts beat as one
Thank you friends

See how I enter my day
With kindness

Caring Hands

Nice crisp morning with

Little chickadees and nuthatches

Hopping in my hand

Eyes revealing trust and love

Lifting wings of grateful praise

Now, if only humans could learn

To trust and love each other

There would be far less pain

Heaven's light would not shine in vain

Manners

When a red-breasted nuthatch, a boreal chickadee,
and a black-capped chickadee approach the seed saucer at
the same time, with his long sharp beak protruding the
nuthatch always runs up and goes first. Even if the
chickadees are already sitting on edge of saucer, the
nuthatch will charge and scare them away. But if a dark-
eyed junco is sitting on saucer calmly eating, he/she ignores
the charge, and the nuthatch waits his turn. The junco is
larger, but even if a chickadee fluffs feathers and looks
twice bigger than the nuthatch, the little nuthatch keeps
charging and wins. This observation comes from a decade
of carefully watching them.

In the chain of evolution, we are all connected and
interrelated. What can we learn from this bird behavior that
moves creation toward beauty, and nurtures gentle
compassion for all of life?

Thinking Like a Bird—

I have been using some of my time

in social isolation from humans

learning to think like birds.

Assessing their emotional feelings

by observing their body language.

What about color of clothing?

I started by thinking gray or brown,

an Ent, a Tolkien walking and talking tree!

The birds had not read Tolkien's treatise.

Reddish orange vest yesterday—

Red-breasted nuthatches loved it!

Five dozen photos of them eating

from my hand proves it.

Not the chickadees.

Today a yellow and grey vest—

Yoink! Yoink! Yeet! Yeet!

Chickadee game is on!

I could have gotten hundreds

of photos, instead of fifty!

Chickadees love sun
An old scarecrow having fun
Makes for nice day

It belongs to the goodness of the world,
that its settled order should
deal tenderly with the faint discordant light
of the dawn of another age.
   —Alfred North Whitehead

My patience paid off
Nuthatches and chickadees
Eating from my hand
Deepens my understanding
Of tenderness and care for all

In retirement, I have spent the last decade
Closely observing birds while walking
in the beauty of Alaska, and tending my feeders
for sunflower heart seeds. One day alone,
I got pictures from my deck of Steller's jays,
magpies, downy and hairy woodpeckers,
dark-eyed juncos of many colors,
boreal and black-capped chickadees,
white-crowned and orange-crowned warblers,
Wilson's warbler, red-breasted nuthatches,
and savannah sparrow. Also saw
numerous water foul on walk around
a lake, plus eagles and ravens soaring
in the blue sky.

In addition to enjoying their beautiful songs,
I have observed that their body language
is all temperament and emotion. One could
almost say, I have learned what it is like
to be a bird. To closely observe and know them
is to measure their feelings.

Searching for Answers

I spent over a dozen years in college and seminary
discovering questions and searching for answers. Questions
grow for years, and we should not expect quick easy
answers. Some questions have the ring of centuries chiming
in them. For example, Pilate asked Jesus at his trial—

"What is truth?" (John 18:38).

Since first encountering this question in seminary,
I have been a question mark
walking in shoes, or maybe fishing waders
pulled up to my rib cage and snuggly strapped on—
A walking question. What is truth?

I have known some people who were answers
walking in house slippers.
They lived with soft easy answers that gave comfort. I run
from these easy answer persons!

>Understanding the question—
>What is truth!

>I am always trying to find an answer.
>What is truth ?
>What shape?
>Where are the answers anyway?

>I wake everyday thinking,
>Today I will find truth.
>I see a glorious sunrise, My soul trembles in awe—
>Is this truth?

I touch a dimple
on my grandchildren's sweet face,
brief smiles as warm as
the earth's sun rise—
Is this truth?

After driving the grandkids to school
I take a long walk in the Chugach mountains.
Wild flowers and chickadees
brighten my way— Is this truth?

I remember Jesus' words:
God cares for the birds of the air
and the flowers of the fields.
God cares for you and me.

All day I walk at the edge
of knowing truth—
looking, longing, touching,
in beauty, goodness, and love.

Looking for truth.
Maybe I will never know for sure
what truth is,
but this day feels like an answer!

"Hope is the thing with feathers
that perches in the soul...
        —Emily Dickinson

Messengers of Hope

As I recline for my daily nap,
in solace of contemplative mood,
chickadees flash in yoga poses.
Fill my heart with joy of gratitude.
Fear dissolves in heaven's peaceful care.
Eyes close in renewed hope and love.

When words become unclear,
I shall focus with photographs.
    —Ansel Adams

Chickadees,
symbol of good fortune,
are one of my favorite birds.
These poses speak poetry.

Nuthatches eating
Sunflower heart seeds from hand
Caring for birds is grand

I had a steady flow of nuthatches
eating from my hand this morning.
I could have gotten a hundred photos.
When I am sitting in my Cracker Barrel rocker
eight feet away from seed saucers, many
varieties of
birds visit: black-capped and boreal
chickadees,
dark-eyed juncos, magpies, Steller's jays,
orange-crowned sparrows, downy
woodpeckers,
pine siskin, and in the silver birch 20 feet
away,
a white-crowned sparrow.
Yes, caring for birds is grand.
It's almost as though
they know I think they are special.

Chickadees on deck
Show what Alaskans look like
After 7.8 earthquake
And light rain all day long
Not to mention COVID-19 spike

Dwayne Cole

Dwayne Cole

Call me Saint Francis
Feeding chickadees from hand
Bird watching is grand

Hope in a Time of Fear

Look at the birds in the sky!
God cares for them,
and God cares for you.
(Based on Matthew 6:26).

Black-capped chickadees
eat sunflower heart seeds
from my hand.

I worked all summer
to gain their trust.

To capture the intimacy
of this experience,
Placed camera on tripod 8 feet away.
Described the action like this:

Wireless remote clicker
in left hand is slick!
Not even Saint Frances
could pull off this trick!

In response to referring to myself
as greater than Saint Francis,
someone, and I won't say who,
with tongue in cheek,

called me—The Bird Man of Alcatraz,
who loved and cared for canaries
nesting in his prison cell.
Our friends keep us humble!

Jesus' gentle teachings say,
God cares for the birds
and God cares for you and me.

This especially applies to the Bird Man—
Abused as a child,
trapped in poverty and crime.
Treated others as they treated him.

The sparrows visited him.
Heralds from heaven above—
Turned his life around.

My prayer is to serve others
in the Spirit of Jesus,
filled with compassion
for all who suffer.

The communion tray filled
with sunflower heart seeds.
Passing Jesus' love
to little feathered friends.

Wings flap saying,
thanks for caring for us!

Emily Dickinson wrote—

Hope is the thing with feathers
that perches in the soul.

The many birds visiting my deck
bring hope to me
in times of stress and fear.

They also inspire me
to write poems like this haiku—

> One little chickadee
> drives away many big fears
> Brings renewed hope

Kindness is everything!

Saint Francis said,
It is in giving that we receive.

Showing compassion
for God's creatures
leads to showing kindness
to all of God's creation.

This includes all persons.
Kindness is reciprocal,
gathering the light of heaven
and warming all in its glow.

Coronavirus
Causing us to fall on knees
A good place to be

One touch of nature
makes us all kin.

(So far I have only convinced the black-capped chickadees
and red-breasted nuthatches of our kinship. Eager to see if
my favorite redpolls will trust me when they come back
around in flocks of 50-100. Getting older and more
wrinkled, they may just see me as a scarecrow and light all
over me. Probably more accurate than calling me Saint
Francis or Bird Man of Alcatraz. I did win the redpolls
trust. I have a picture of them lighting all over my arm and
hand, filled with seeds. Also Steller's jays eat peanuts from
my hand.)

Eyes of Hope

Sparkling bird eyes
Reveal mystery of universe
Strike fire in the heart
Bring tears of compassion
Kindle love for all humankind

(Remember to wash seed dishes often,
as well as hands before and after feeding.)

Red yellow black and white

All human races are revealed

In colors within nature photos

The desire for all to be fed

All to be touched with tenderness

Shines in these rhymes

"Hope is the thing with feathers"

as Emily Dickinson discovered

in her garden of contemplation

Strikes fire in the heart
Lights a flame in our soul

Nurtures healing in the universe

Sunflower heart seeds
Chickadees come to the table
Angel wings say thanks

The sun rose this morning
As chickadees knew it would
Licked up candy-cane mountain.

Chickadees are viewed positively
by many Native American cultures.
In Cherokee mythology
the chickadee is a symbol of truth and
knowledge,
and the arrival of a chickadee is thought
to warn of coming danger
and foretell the future.
In many Plains Indian tribes,
chickadees are also
symbols of success.
It is considered good luck
to see or hear one,
especially in a dream or vision.
Seeing their beauty and grace
one can believe this and more.
I am happy just sitting on my deck,
and watching them eat my sunflower seeds,
with an Alpenglow sunrise in background.

Chickadees catch fire
Life will never be the same
My soul draws flame
Moses' burning bush
Holy! Holy! Holy!

Love my chickadees
Messengers of good news
Love is in the air

Cupid's arrow
Aimed at your heart
Love is coming

COVID rages across the world,
Church bells are silent.

Doors closed to worshipers,
Bibles remain in pew racks.

Black-capped chickadees visit me,
Harbingers of hope.

One of the greatest needs in our modern world
is to cultivate a reverence for life.

God values all life and feels within God's own being all
lives. If God values us, we can value all others.

Conclusion

Good News Tanka

At some glad moment
Was it Mother Nature's choice
To give birds a song
Black-capped chickadees sing
All nature joins the chorus

Simple acts of loving kindness
to our self, our family,
and to all living things
are the most hopeful
and powerful transformers
in the world. Dwayne Cole

Snowman with blackcap
chickadees are top notch fun
wouldn't you agree

Little chickadees

Sing the music of my soul

God cares for us all

Chickadee Sonnet

Black-capped chickadees are such fun.
Intent on stashing winter seeds.
Feathers of hope, illumined by the sun.
Snowfall has just begun indeed.

Gather as many as you wish.
Devour to meet your needs.
High on my list is filling your dish
with sunflower heart seeds.

I'll never forget the wondrous feeling
the first time you landed in my hand.
You sent my heart reeling.

As long as you keep lighting in my hand,
I will write poems of love and kindness.
Your love is as true as a wedding band.

BEAUTY AND KINDNESS TRAINING EXERCISE

The central purpose of this book is about growing in beauty and kindness. Poetry of beauty and kindness is relational. Life is about relationships from birth till death. Relational beauty and kindness come naturally in family and community, and flows in personal ways. Emphasizing the relational aspects of beauty broadens the definition, moving toward kindness.

Mindfully setting aside times to meditate on how we can better show beauty and kindness can help us become more sensitive and responsive to others within our everyday circles and move to include all persons.

Find a quiet time each day to contemplate on what you desire for your family and yourself:

* To be safe and secure
* To be happy and at peace
* To have good health
* To be free from fear
* To have fun times for all in family
* To see beauty in all people, animals, and all living things

A Summary Vision of Beauty

My vision for the world is that it move toward beauty.
Seeing beauty in nature is a step in that direction.

Beauty is the key for understanding
the loving and generous heart beat of nature.

The inner nourishing of a kind spirit in every person is
one of the most important needs in our world today.

Beauty in one's heart is felt by the universe.

Yet, I am painfully aware of the chasm between this
vision and its ultimate expression in our world that is so
divided.

Visions may be expressed in gentle words,
but they are more powerful when expressed in tender
actions.

Centered in beauty and kindness We can transform our
world.

Nature's Miracle

One reason for playing with chickadee beauties is so
the joy you see in them will become your joy and
their beauty will become your beauty.

The sense of being
one with chickadee beauty
is Mother Nature's gift.

Chickadee beauty is nature laughing
with us, while moving us toward Peace.

Oh the joy of spring
Birds in flight
Warmer days you bring
My soul's delight

BOOKS BY DWAYNE COLE

A Center that Holds: Adventures in Kindness

Alpenglow Miracles: Fire Dance of Wonder

A Prayer of Blessing: As You Go Remember This

A Relational Hermeneutic of Kindness

A Relational Trinity of Kindness

BEARS AND MOOSE OF ALASKA: Nature Poetry

Black-capped Chickadees: Messengers of Hope

Clouds of Inspiration

Down on the Farm in Georgia: A Poetic Memoir

Dragonfly Magic

Gentle Galilean Glories: The Tender Teachings of Jesus

God and Evil: An Ode to Kindness

Heart Haiku: Alaska Inspired Photos and Poems

Heart Sijo: Alaska Inspired Photos and Poems

Jesus' Transforming Beatitudes: Selected Sermons from Year A

Jesus' Transforming Love: Selected Sermons from Year B

*Jesus' Transforming Gentle Teachings: Selected Sermons from Year C
Kindness Is Every Step*

Lone Leaf Dancing

Poems Inspired by Process Philosophy

Poet of the Universe: A Vision of Beauty and Goodness.

Rainbows of Hope

Snowshoe Hare Beauty

The Apostles' Creed: A Living Creed for the Living Church.

The Bible: A Poetic Journey

The Book of Revelation: Jesus' Kindness Transforms Suffering

The Serenity Prayer: A Pathway to Peace and Happiness

*The Story of the Bible: Authority, Inspiration, Canonization,
Translation*

TREES AND DRIFTWOOD: Poetic Ecology

When Flowers Speak, Listen

When Stones Speak

WINGS OF INSPIRATION

Parson's Porch Books

Black-Capped Chickadees: Messengers of Good News
ISBN: Softcover 978-1-960326-75-1
Copyright © 2024 by Dwayne Cole

Parson's Porch Books is an imprint of Parson's Porch & Company (PP&C) in Cleveland, Tennessee. PP&C is a self-funded charity which earns money by publishing books of noted authors, representing all genres. Its face and voice is **David Russell Tullock** (dtullock@parsonsporch.com).

Parson's Porch & Company *turns books into bread & milk* by sharing its profits with the poor.

www.parsonsporch.com